UNDERGROUND FACILITY

UNDERGROUND FACILITY

C. E. J. Simons

ISOBAR
PRESS

First published in 2018 by

Isobar Press
14 Isokon Flats, Lawn Road,
London NW3 2XD, United Kingdom
&
Sakura 2-21-23-202, Setagaya-ku,
Tokyo 156-0053, Japan

http://isobarpress.com

ISBN 978-4-907359-24-9

ACKNOWLEDGEMENTS

Poems in this volume have previously appeared in *A Tower Miscellany* (Oxford: Tower Poetry, 2010), *The Bridport Prize Anthology* 2016, the Cinnamon Press *Sequences* anthology shortlist (2010), *The Keats-Shelley* Prize 2005, *The May Anthologies* 2003, *The May Anthologies* 2004, *Oxford Poetry*, and *World Haiku*.

COVER IMAGE

Laurent Grasso. *Studies into the Past.*
Oil on Wood, 45 x 35 cm. Private collection.
Courtesy of the Artist and the Edouard Malingue Gallery.

To
F. E. R. S.
K. J. S.
and F. E. S.

...bid the dishonest man mend himself; if he mend, he is no longer dishonest; if he cannot, let the botcher mend him. Any thing that's mended is but patched: virtue that transgresses is but patched with sin; and sin that amends is but patched with virtue.

— *Twelfth Night*

One must at every opportunity use the subterranean paths of action and thought, erase the traces, appear suddenly and irrelevantly, endlessly conquer oneself, never hesitate to sodomize one's soul so that it will be reborn purer and stronger than ever.

— from *The Secret Life of Salvador Dali*

Why, this is Paradise — we are in Paradise, or at least under it.

— Gene Wolfe, *The Claw of the Conciliator*

Contents

III. LIFE SCIENCES

AFTERLIVES

FRESH BREATH

comes and goes.
Now it comes just as

this menthol lozenge –
a bezelled gem

of artificial orange
the wrapper calls *midnight juice* –

on which I've
been sucking hard

to preserve
what's left of my voice

has been reduced
to a shard –

to the exact size,
shape, and hardness

of a loose
incisor

A PIECE OF THE VICTORY

i.

The war was obviously won, but the powers-that-be
refused to demob my grandfather Davy,

a conscripted mathematician
who'd taught the gunners from Labrador

how, like Prince Hal's longbowmen
you could use a parabola

to put an ash-shaft through a chevalier's eye
or knock a Heinkel or a Junkers out of the sky

like Merlin with a magic missile.
As he hung around the ruins

of Portsmouth, they put him to work
between decks in the No. 2 dry dock,

crawling through close quarters, thick with the odour
            of tar;
put him to work with protractor

and slide rule,
not rebuilding the town, but resuming the restoration

of HMS *Victory* –
scarred by the Blitz, but intact, the epitome

of the irony of collateral damage,
a frippery that managed

to survive a hit from one of the bombs
that were shattering babies in their mothers' arms.

She was crumbling away in her dock
like a neglected council tower block,

ribs cracked, boards split
by time and not by Messerschmitt.

As they stripped away the decaying English oak
to make way for the harder but more brittle

post-colonial
teak and iroko

my granddad, poker-faced, pocketed a piece –
a piece of the structural weakness –

some shard of a beam or brace.
It stands next to a photo of him on my bookcase:

an underfed, piano-wire man.
He told me Henry Tudor trussed

acres of English oak to warp them curved –
to hydrodyne, to outface any sea. I must

still take him as I took him, at his word.
So my folks – Welsh-Canadian folk,

doubly dominioned
trussed me like old Henry grew a rib-oak:

green-pinioned
but strong enough for a sea-fence,

strong enough to weather the turbulence
of these and other legends.

ii.

And he, standing there in the ruins –
the tough, mischievous mathematician

conscripted for air defence,
conscripted to make a magic wall of shrapnel

against bombers sighting
the dome of St Paul's,

and passing down shards of stories
as much as practical geometry

to his descendants:
what would he think

of his grandson's civil defence
of a wholly impractical existence?

Could he imagine his skills extinct
in two generations?

That he'd engineer a grandson
not to be functional

but surreal, a godawful
formlessness, unless you count

a sort of lyric form – which he wouldn't?
What would he have thought,

figuring a square root,
to know that in the end, what I'd compute

were no curves to restore a flagship's prow,
not even the curve of an English longbow –

or – to warp the metaphor –
just the rounded maple

for the back-wood of a wincing lute,
not enough for an airframe, or a cello,

just a boy bent
on self-making,

on the pleasures of effacement,
and the whims of getting it wrong,

less a sea-fence than a Cnut,
less a *Victory* than an icebound *Resolute*

crushed into the Arctic's odd angles –
incalculably bent on song?

A SALVATION ARMY BOYHOOD

'Love stood before me
in that place
prayers could not lure me
to Christ's house'
           — Geoffrey Hill, 'A Pentecost Castle'

I came to as a citizen
draped in a flag of two blood oxygen levels –
arterial and venal –
ringing the lemon airburst of a sun.

During the sermon, I'd bow my head
over a yellow Junior Soldier sketchpad
drawing Joshua or Samson aiming a heat-ray
at Soviet infantry

while my unconscious sipped the sermon's precepts:
always confess; always give others more and yourself less.
I tried – but kept rationing the loaves, the fishes,
multiplying selfishness with selfishness.

The fabric of the church, the so-called citadel
was built to outlast any cathedral:
a concrete bunker, with a plaque kept in good kelter
declaring it a designated fall-out shelter.

Between the pancake brunches for the homeless,
the drunks sprawling like Bosch's St Jerome,
and reports of ss-25 test launches,
a church basement became a home.

My grandfather had made the cross
of lacquered Manitoba spruce
that hung on the curved wall of the bandstand-shell
like a spy satellite, weightless.

Between my paper spy-planes' parabols
and the rustle of my Marvel comics
those wooden crosshairs, that band-shell's concave lens
focused the atomic

rays of the dolorous euphonium
into my blood, transmuting the reflected
words from the pulpit into wild mutations –
the pipes of Euterpe, the horns of Triton –

while dead Apollo strummed my blue blood red:
a pulmonary vein pumping the stuff
of myth into my faith's slow circulations –
the faith I've found, and never found enough.

SAMSON

i.

You're shaving my head
as you've done for twenty years,

pruning me prudently
to keep us hedged

against my barbers'
exorbitant fees,

and I'm thinking of the seven oiled curls
of the snoring Nazirite

snaking to the sand
from the hands of a servant girl –

hands shaking with each scissor-snip
by the light of her Black Ops

starlight scope,
the sweet-almond tang

of toxic Macassar
foreshadowing a massacre.

The servant trims, the wife distracts below
with mouthed

thanks to Dagon,
god of the plough

for her big man's
hypersomnia.

She's unbraided the challah
of his loincloth

as the sharp shadow-puppets
of a midnight buzz-cut

dance in the thin flame
of the chiragh,

followed by the satisfying rasp
of oiled razor-scrapes –

they're taking no chances here,
not by the breadth of one stray super-hair.

ii.

And I think again
as I have these twenty years

(as your fingers
turn me, turn me, or lift my chin)

that for Samson,
for once, it wasn't

the blowfly-buzz of the salon
or the heat of the styling irons

or the howls of the Philistine hit squad
that finally woke him up,

but that dream of death:
that nightmare

of feeling your hair
fall out in the mirror –

clump under
invisible razor-strokes

and drop.
Like him I'd felt the thrilling danger

of going it alone;
and the panic of losing my edge,

or worse, what kept it honed:
the soft but shaping strop

of the death-gasp,
the almost constant combat.

Samson woke with a sharp breath
as I did, once, in the darkness of total loss,

at the sudden, exquisite
absence of God –

consumed with despair
for the loss of his hair,

an existential baldness
beyond medical help.

Not like me, relieved to feel it –
that lightness of the scalp.

Under the ram-horned galaxies,
under the red-eye of the war-god's hangover,
needle in the red, in the middle of nowhere,
in the overleaf of a new financial year
I first came to in the back seat of a car.

In the middle of Manitoba's section lines,
in the middle of the dead blue of an April night,
out of the blue, with Elton John in the charts,
half a world away from any holt or heath
I entered the world dead blue, by the skin of my teeth.

On the open range, with Zephyrus free to blow
from Banff to Thunder Bay without interruption,
blowing black cloudburst and canola-yellow,
on the yellowed suede of a second-hand Mercury Comet
my father rubbed me until I had some comment.

With the red coals of an omen – the crossing signal
still red – the grain cars still trundling past,
with all the luck on the wrong side of the tracks
Zeus toweled off my tracklement and treacle
and puffed my trachea with a ruddy gust.

My parents couldn't know the violence they'd unleashed
halfway through their race to the hospital;
how could they guess their chain reaction of flesh
would choke on odes, leave elegies unfinished,
would rather die red and raging than die dull?

All this comes back to me, locked in a bronze crock:
I've been against the grain since that dawn's pink,
and every grain the gods reaped, I've repaid
with misery, with mayhem and crusade,
with chain-gun cannon-fire and carrion-stink.

You think this lead-lined womb contains my fission
better than prison, or never being born?
The grain god's harvest fills the war god's tank
and fuels the pounding fists inside this urn:
you can bottle me up but I'll always return.

ASHCASH

for J. B.

Hedging his bets, never one to be caught short,
my father-in-law retired to the estate
of a zero-hours contract as an undertaker's mate:
a growth industry, even in this climate
he said, as they measured him for his tails and top hat –
suiting him to his late profession
as one of death's impeccably dressed dustmen.

Nitrated by the dead,
his East London slang germinated,
sprouted nightshade and wolfsbane:
mourners were *grizzlers*, sobbing or gargoyle-grim
behind the hearse.
Vicars slid into the oven doing *St Peter's handstand*,
the privilege of clergy – i.e. headfirst.
And the two medics lucky enough
to double-check that every stiff's a stiff
got their *ashcash* – the palms of their latex gloves greased
with a hundred-and-eighty-five quid apiece.

Money for old rope, my father-in-law said.
And I thought of another kind of ashcash: his own fee,
paid cash in hand, but a pittance –
less than an obol for a much longer journey –
and after he'd learned the ropes – the lines and sheets
in death's ever-expanding corporate fleet.

He'd mastered the secrets of the sacred hoist
despite his arthritis and a bum knee,
with as much an air of dignity

as the Eternal Footman would expect –
going the extra mile
for the fallen rank and file

like his unobserved respects
paid to a nameless biddy,
when not a soul came
down the crem to claim her remains
or mourn her council-issued urn's descent:
no obsequies, no cerement,

just four white-haired men
like waxworks in the rain –
count them off – *Lear, Gloucester, Albany, Kent* –
bareheaded in the silence
of a more than Christian reverence,

not grudging their pittance
of ashcash, not noticing the old church clock
was running slow – as slow and sure as hemlock:
waiting a good while after
that black mouth in the green was sealed –
waiting for that wound, somehow, to be annealed.

NECK VERSE

for Ben Jonson

What can I read you, to spare my life?
What good can my book-learning do you?
I've sold scripts – though the royalties go to the ex-wife –
I know art – I know prose – all that good stuff you value –
I've got four or five languages, at least to a level
my teachers consider 'survival'.

You don't look impressed, up there on your bench.
Look, I know that my rap sheet is more of a book,
and for killing a man, it's not Latin or French
or rhetorical style that gets you off the hook –
but the well-read felon who sobs and repents
is worth more than a capital sentence.

If justice is blind and the talented man
gets treated the same as the yobs and the louts
then he's got no incentive to be better than
those 'worst elements' you complain about –
and I could have spent my best years on the dole
or embezzling your pensions and payrolls.

So let's find a double standard that works for us both.
I'll send your lover sonnets (I know she's hard to please) –
I'll spill all the shortcuts to spiritual growth,
I'll teach your wife yoga and your kids Chinese –
just *ixnay* the gallows and let me become
the one who got off with a brand on his thumb.

KING OF SHADOWS

'Believe me, king of shadows, I mistook.'
– A Midsummer Night's Dream 3.2

I know a bank where the wild times blew
the roof off every IOU
and promissory note. *'Quite over-leveraged'?* –
more like pulled arse-backwards through the hedge
and spider-web of our own securities,
leaving our clients mostly on their knees.
Some nights I bunked down on the trading floor
in those last days when nobody was poor
but the actual poor, clowns with no capital,
and with no balls to take it from the till.
I snoozed, lullabied by a mustard-seed –
a Zopiclone, or a wee Ambien,
or the snaky woodsmoke of a little weed
exhaled into the ventilation system –
by fantasies of a fleet of private jets
financed with margin calls on forex spreads,
or shorting solid small-caps till they cracked,
laying a family business on its back
for me to have my way with what they built –
three generations mortgaged to the hilt.
I slept with my suit coat rolled under my head,
soft as the duck-down of our moral hazard.
And when the snake oil ran a little thin
and the investigation widened,
we weeded the servers, wiped our histories
and dumped our cache of fairy fantasies.
We knew the public purse would make amends,
just like I know those days will come again:
the management will spread a little bling,
press the flesh, juice the buds of spring,

while our analysts and accounting wizards
dance a roundel with the regulators.
We'll run rings around any opposition,
leaving them dazzled, sated, or undone
in the back of a mile-long limousine,
or laid out on some dew-damp public green
staring at the cleavage of our go-to girls
or maddened by the full moon of an eight-ball.
Our sweet Athenian action was a sure
thing – till it wasn't. For the small investor
like yourself – the working woman or man,
or the pensioner with an aggressive plan
for growth – you should have seen the risks, the shadow
lengthening on your fat portfolio.
Rant online that there's one law for
the rich – for capital – and one for labour
if it makes you feel better. You made your bets,
you strutted it, shadowing my calls and puts –
you and your penny-players down the pub
talking so big, but running with the mob,
every man with his *Financial Times*,
every man past it, locked in way sub-prime,
plumber and joiner and low-level crim
each telling your mate that you're one up on him.
Now each of you has got to live with it –
squint through the hangover, take the haircut,
bin your dream of a Costa del Sol retirement
since you (and coastal Spain) are now insolvent –
foreclosed to us. You thought that we were mates
since we talked the talk – the East End, the estates.
But you were never an insider – you were never close –
like the waiter who counts himself a wedding guest –
you couldn't afford my suit with a year's pay.

Cheerio – we've gone to ground, left you to bray
in protest at the terms of your defeat
that are no terms. You are not the elite
and never will be, while we control the cycle
of boom and bust – the price of wheat and wool –
while you hang your limp donkey-ears and squat
like Midas at the bottom of the market,
rated as junk – a human pack-animal –
hating yourself for being so gullible,
and cursing me, who brought you to this pass:
downgraded to the lowest asset class.

EMPUSA RED

after Keats, 'La Belle Dame Sans Merci'

What's up with you my son – alone
an' loi'erin' with a piss-pale ale?
You should be 'ome, not 'oled up 'ere
after last call.

Go on, tell me – what's 'appened to you?
It looks like you died of freezer-burn.
You got a job – a gorgeous wife;
I am ... concerned.

You look right rough – white as a ghost –
a three-day beard – an' mate, you smell
of smoke – an' roses – an' stale sweat
from the arse of 'ell.

'I met this bird...' – *Oh, 'ere we go –*
'down the 'Aycock the other night –
li'l porcelain doll – red 'air to 'er waist –
touchy as dynamite.

Asked me straight off to take 'er 'ome –
said she weren't into no rough stuff
but she got a big four-poster bed
and fur-lined 'andcuffs.'

You berk. 'I drove 'er back to 'ers –
she's got the radio on, she's singin'
'endrix, Joplin, all them 'its
from way back when.

She's got a lovely pad – all red –
bottle of Monopole on ice –
she's mixin' drinks and talkin' French –
pure paradise.

Course I *knew* it were an 'oney trap –
but I couldn't not – I couldn't not –
she made me kiss 'er seven times
in seven spots.

Then the drink I 'ad must a knocked me out
cold as a bag of frozen beans –
I don't remember nothin' but
this dream I dreams:

I saw me dad, an' 'is dad too,
an' 'is – a glowerin' line – all dead –
they moan: *'You done been 'ad by Miss
Empusa Red.'*

I saw me ancestors and sons
all livid – corpsin' to the bone –
an' I came to in a rubbish skip –
no dosh, no phone.

An' that's why I'm sittin' 'ere alone
loi'erin' over a pale ale
freezin', 'arf pissed, 'oled up 'ere while
my marriage fails.

All them tales of *fems fatales* –
them dir'y magic poems an' books –
didn' save me – and won't save you,
despite that look.'

From a distance, I couldn't tell
if her breath was good and gone –
warmth and decay in rapprochement –
or if she was just sleeping well,

snug to the wall, a white-faced ewe.
Or was she tense with fear – was she
immobilized by injury –
too hurt to strain, too scared to move?

Or maybe she was autumn-full,
big with a lamb, tired on the moss,
the wall dulling the sleet-storm's hiss,
keeping its needles off her wool.

Pregnant, or hurt, we'd call it in –
I dropped my pack, loped down the cut
to get a closer look. No rut
had run its course here to fruition

except the rut that splits the fells,
millennium by millennium –
death's too-wide grin, his fleshless gums
ragged and sharp, like fingernails.

The dead sheep's second life had just
begun to set in, staring out
from empty sockets: rapid rot,
the rest intact – her grey fleece brushed

with pearls, a patch of frosty soil
thawed for the planting, soil so moist
a spade could make an easy thrust
socket-deep into her bowels,

into that red mould, just past life,
that takes life as its root and pulse:
a spring in any season – skulls
that don't grin at your joy, or grief,

but at their trick of distancing –
the way her white face drew me close
down the red bracken to my loss
of wonder at the work of spring.

Whether they're sheltering royalty or riffraff,
the nomads celebrate the butchery
of a sheep or goat in a banquet on behalf
of their guests – a banquet consisting entirely

of numbles
and sausages made from onions and blood.
We sit, guest-humbled
on the edge of the youngest daughter's bed

wondering whether the setting sun
will spice to taste, or cast a curse
on the rising lumps in the witch's cauldron
so ceremoniously set before us –

as if Banquo or Saul
had learned their fate
from a machine-pressed aluminium bowl
brimming with more peculiar meat

than bats or frogs
or the thumbs of pilots.
Whenever you start to gag
I thrust my hands into the pot

and, loudly as I can, pipe up
on the probabilities
of my next lucky dip:
that I loved the lungs and kidneys

but haven't yet had some heart.
At worst, it's a savage ritual
from a savage time, from a world athwart
the distinction between 'food' and 'animal' –

at best, it's training for a diplomat's feast –
but much of the world would still maintain
that you can gain the powers of any beast
by making a meal of it. So, in that vein,

setting my culture aside, I'll root around
in the lukewarm blood-broth
for less than a pound of flesh, less than half a pound
that tastes of certain uncouth

secretions and tissues:
an unusual organ with a fluid shape –
a vestigial organ, of no use
to any man but a man of my type.

I tracked down the boatswain
who'd manned us home from Tunis.
He was running anchovies and Calvados
between Bruges and Genoa
in a rotting caravel. A crew of degenerates. Nine rusty guns.
He's the man for the job: the job, and then the noose.
The other one's dead – the master of the flagship –
what was it – the *Bohemia*? The *Hydra*?
But dead, these four years. Some sea-fight off Aleppo.

Before I left that island full of music,
vexed to my bones, my world picture in turmoil,
I made certain calculations, by eyeball and instrument,
by compass and quadrant;
took windward and leeward samples of soils and plants.
And I did it hush-hush – made sure I wasn't observed,
except by the winds and tides, the palms and birds –
which, given the isle's unusual properties,
as I measured them were no doubt measuring me.

When we reach the coordinates
no one but the boatswain and I expect
anything but a patch of empty sea. The island's gone.
Equanimity's a curse on those who live too long.
I'm plotting a course on to Bermuda
when the ship's boy drags me up to the deck,
insisting he saw something big pass overhead.
By'r lakin, sir, a spirit! A giant bird.
Did the boy see a roc? Or a *garuda*?

I strain my eyes up at the Bear –
there's nothing there.
Only the new moon, freighting the old.
And why should I expect a miracle?
He owed me nothing, the old Duke of Milan,
for the way I played both sides, keeping my own hand
hidden. What did I do for him and his baby girl
but keep the usurper from cutting their throats outright –
give them food and water, and leave them to the pirates?

My fate's the sentence of the Machiavel
who served whomever happened to seize the tiller.
I was charitable – *that* was never hard –
but I never intervened, and I still don't.
These waters seethe with migrants:
a stew of half-scuttled boats escorted
by overloaded inflatables, by cried-out coastguard,
a sea of flags and flares I ordered my crew to ignore
to get us here before we went down ourselves.

The rotting carcasses bloat,
swelling and deflating with the tides
of wars, pandemics, and the ebbing coffers
of states that I helped fail. A face-down toddler
stays face-down, on a beach where I once kissed
the jewelled pincers of dictator's wives.
I've left more than one child adrift in a leaky boat,
and whatever spirit that just did a flypast knows this.
I should have done more. I should have done much more.

The ant was found out for his formications,
the bee censured for 'hive mentality,'
maggots and grubs for warring in Dead Earnest,
Drosophila for exploiting their mutations,
Benchuca bugs for the best of Darwin's theory.

Others were sentenced for lewd exhibitions –
the tarantúla for the *tarantella*,
the cockroach for the *loco cucaracha*,
the dung beetle for playing with old feces,
some moths for bestial impersonations.

Blowflies went down for touting cuts of meat
left in the sun, long past their sell-by dates,
scarabs were blamed for Tutankhamen's curse,
wood ticks for smuggling themselves in on tourists,
black widows for scamming the wedding registry.

Butterflies got nicked for tempting Trader Stein
to net all nature's symmetry for the kill-jar,
fleas for actual bestiality,
bed bugs for a lack of taste in furniture,
termites for the reverse. But the worst fine

fell on the unassuming Brown Recluse:
that small arachnid's gross temerity
to exhibit no distinguishing features
save for its snug home, and its deadliness.
It went down for being like all other creatures.

TWO POEMS FROM THE MUSEUM OF MAN AND
NATURE, WINNIPEG

1. *Fur Press*

With the help of the screw-press, these fur-bales –
Hudson Bay's treasure-heaps, its brush and bristle,
long breathless in the museum's lull –
have packed to strike east for the St. Lawrence,
for the blood-lullaby
to rock them in holds across the sea,
getting used to the hard-pressed intimacy
of this mock fur-house, of each other.
Nobody waves, nobody weeps:
the children are bound up with the parents.

From my childhood's gruesome machines –
the guillotine, the Apega of Nabis, or the bed
where the Paris gamblers were smothered –
it has become, if not benign,
cousin to the wine-press of the Aegean,
far from the bear-coats of Budapest
and the felt beavers of London:
as if all it pressed were the lacustrines of Lake Agassiz –
as if all it pressed were the pelt of the soil.
As if the blood of my economy were wine.

2. *Diorama: Prairie Settlers in a Sod House,* 1900

It's as if when the Manitoban prairie
was rolled out plain
by the Pleistocene's
slow rolling-pin,
one bump remained –

one hump in the mile-deep soil,
cut with axe, spade, and trowel –
turf walls stacked like sacks of flour.
The ruddy cheek of a peat fire –
the rocking of an improbable cradle –
three and a dog hunkered down for the night
under the wind's inconsolable
hiss and howl:
I tell you, I tell you, I tell you
this place is uninhabitable.

Let's have a peek in.
It's as real as those first few days
after the falling-out with heaven:
the wind's saw-teeth working their way between
new-settled flesh and old ideas of sin.

At this point, there's no such thing
as a raw deal. There's only what still is:
and midwinter, there's hardly
the scrawl of a line of tamarack
or the full stop of a black stone
on the unbroken whiteness
of a permanent contract.

Half-smothered by the prairie's white embrace,
they're slumbering on a golden hoard:
the coming century's harvests
of wheat so rich Demeter will confess
the sweat of the human face
has left her lost for words.

Their lullaby's in the wind's relentless sermon
and the mumbled voice
of the plough and the butter-churn,
the squeal of the Red River Cart
and the chatter of the spinning jenny:
Eden on its own could only feed so many.

GHOST WRITER

for Stephen Fry

The power-lunchers swap each other's books
with a nonchalant *here's mine* and *who did yours?*
while we raise glasses to our agents' cheers
and struggling poets shoot us bitter looks.

Politicians, archbishops and pop idols,
footballers, faded reality stars:
I've leaned across my pad to catch their scandals
and craft them into bestselling memoirs.

Homo rhetoricus, my working model
still holds that last *matryoshka,* that last doll
secreted in its nested lacquer shells:
the bitter pill, the irreducible

aniseed lure on which my readers suck.
Competitors, so quick to call it luck
would find my methods quite unorthodox:
Ouija boards, ectoplasm, pendulum clocks,

half-silvered mirrors, a spirit cabinet,
the music of a bell inside a bell jar –
the fraudster's apparatus proves adept
at raising subjects for a real ghost writer.

But Limbo never held my interest –
its tales so long, its ghosts so virtuous.
Instead I sussed out where Lord Lucan's bones are
and who shagged this or that prime minister.

Who was your source? the cocktail minxes purr.
My Alfa Romeo, my fine Mont Blanc –
I shake my head, and take their mobile numbers.
I could have been a poet and a drunk.

Maybe I liked the work – not anymore.
I write at midnight, peering through smoked glass,
taking dictation from these tapping bores,
testy that all things passed have never passed.

You think the dead appreciate the scum
I've skimmed from Hell and Purgatory's ghettoes?
People still moaning when their time has come
didn't contribute much. And I should know –

I've spilt my ink on libellous offenses.
My ghosts whine I'm a lame amanuensis
for trying to improve on what they've said –
not every author's better when they're dead.

LIVE FEED

HAIKU

Wrecked on a dry shore
I crack a chunk of feldspar
and find an oyster.

This oyster's my youth:
a slurried tale, but still fresh
in its brine of truth.

I.

Bring me
the live feed.
Bring me a dozen
hearts in canopic jars. Crack the porcelain
at the exact moment Osiris revives them.
Bring me no clankers.
Bring me no
closed
dead.

Don't wreck
them with flourishes
of Tabasco or garlic –
these virgins in white petticoats,
these sterile virgins, petrified mid-flout:
just a little *mignonette*
helps you hang on to the half-second before
their own cold bathwater
eases them down
your throat

2.

i. *Seduction*

Those student days –
oysters were the only pearls
I could buy her.
A couple of dozen
of what Pepys bought by the barrel
wouldn't leave us beggars.
Or would they?

The Muscadet –
'in no way objectionable,
and in no way fine'
slipped a silver band
round what they used to call the 'temple',
round my *os sphenoidale* –
slipped a silver tongue
like a slip of pickled *kohada*
behind my teeth.
And if that wasn't enough
false courage,
her smile made me bold:
here's poison, and here's gold.

ii. *Conciliation*

After a spat
(maybe it's our anniversary)
I take her for oysters,
make her a peace offering
of a dozen kingdoms of solipsism.

Each animal, lying there in his brack,
offers the soft pearl of himself – love-spent, slack –
to the vacuum of her lips.

Each hermit will in turn
slip through his own lumen,
and prove luminous:

call her mistress, and salute her
with his last slide (burial at sea)
as she garnishes, lifts, tips.

3.

        Speaking of oysters, Swift said,
He was a bold man
that first ate one –
                but I'd bet a string
                of pearls it was a woman: an exiled queen

or a starving beach-girl
            in Tarsus, or Miteline –

        fatherless Marina
                  with nothing
but the will to live, to beat brothel and cloister –
a will beyond the pales –

        making her beachhead
armed with nothing but a sackful of oysters

and her bleeding fingernails.

4.

In their opalescent paddling pools,
their millionaire finger-bowls,
the oysters wait, supine,
awed by visions of the angelic shoals.

Then down they go, one by one.
Another carapace for the garden:
feed for the white roses of Balin
and the silver roses of Balan,

each knight's tarnished armour
scattered with eggshells and coffee-grounds
to fertilise the rubies
of a hot-pepper vine.

Exuent exoskeletons.
Sluice another clatter
of hide-scrapers
on the shell-midden.

A twist in the plot: the victim
was also the murder weapon.

5.

Professor Pequod, naturalist *emeritus*
goes on at me about the glorious limitations
of bivalves, of arthropods and crustaceans.

Not the gastropods – he views them with suspicion.
I have a recurring nightmare
he confesses, swabbing at his spectacles' half-moons
in which a sea-snail the size of the Millennium Dome
slithers up out of the Thames
and lays waste to the Docklands.

He's equally suspicious of humans –
a species condemned
to carry their china shards
deep down: cages and spars
of apatite
hidden in the red plush
of their ventriloquized meat.

No shucking off of exoskeletons for us.
No rebirth from tank-plate to baby skin –
meaning, to Pequod, the catastrophe
of no limitations
on our growth;
of not having to deal with a lifetime
crawling around in our own coffins.

6.

And after we slurp down the first half-dozen
in reverential silence

I have to open my big mouth
wider than professor or Prioress

would find polite (part your lips
prudently – this isn't fish and chips –

as shallowly as you can to inhale
the living liquid from its grail).

And I start holding forth
on oyster-legend and oyster-lore –

how the Iroquois used a sharpened oyster shell
to sever Father Laforgue's thumb –

how the pearl-oyster's bothered, not by a grain of sand,
but a parasite in its epithelium

though in Mikimoto's pearl-farms, his pearl-oysters were fed
a bit of their own lip, complete with lip-piercing –

how we too have a few grains
of sand in our brains –

how pearl oysters
aren't really oysters at all –

and how in a trick meeting
between pearl oysters and oysters for eating,

Alice and the Walrus
couldn't have guessed

that in 1907
the oyster-grafting needle

that would render natural pearls
inferior to artificial

would be patented in Mie Prefecture
by a carpenter.

(All this holding forth
being one source

of all these make-up meals,
as it will be for 'the foreseeable'

as it will be till
I learn my lesson –

as it will be until,
over oysters and wine

I learn to be the man
who says less than

enough, and just *for God's sake* kisses her
when she needs to be kissed –

until I learn to hold my tongue
in its enamel stirrups –

until I learn to keep *shtum* –
to clam,

as it were,
up.)

7.

i. *Pandora*

Though the shape of the oyster varies according to the bottom to which it's attached, it always grows with its fluted side up: a lidded chalice, a Pandora's box, held shut from the inside by sheer demon-will – as if all that evil, turned introvert, wanted nothing more to do with the world.

ii. *Apnœa*

A young pearl-diver from Miyajima greased herself in pork fat,
clipped her nose with a tortoiseshell *pince-nez*, and tumbled
out of her coracle, gripping a beach-boulder to sink her.
She filled her basket with oysters and mussels, but
passed out while resurfacing. She would have
drowned, but the boulder that took her to the
bottom was no boulder, but a sleeping sea-turtle.
It caught her as she sank, and carried
her to an undersea cave at the mouth
of the Yomi. In the cave was a palace
ruled by a pirate prince, the bastard
son of Tethys and Susa-no-O.
The prince showed the pearl-
diver that each of her

oysters

when tickled open
underwater, unfurled living
sea-feathers. From these he made
four wings for her: two for the sea, and
two for the air. But, though he married her,
the prince refused to live with her. *Some
men.* He led her through the secret sea-caves
of the world to the Antarctic Ocean. Now half
the year she spends flying with the albatross,
keeping them out of trouble, and half the year she spends
swimming with sea turtles, teaching them the difference
between jellyfish and plastic. She does a lot of good. And she
and the prince have many sea-children – all nameless, all loved.

But of course, her mortal body remains dead.

8.

This oyster's not an oyster,
but a thought. The reverse –
that this thought of an oyster
is no thought
but an oyster –
may also be the case.

If a case then the accusative,
an object without a subject:
if a thought then the eighth,
if the eighth, then *une huître*:
a thought like mercury fulminate,
like the antidote to saltpetre.

9.

Champagne is what we need –
fetch it directly
as the oyster-guzzling wankers used to say.
Champagne and more champagne – the spume
of careless days. Sea-foam to crest
these rocks of the sea.

There's a whitewashed house
by a river, couched in a field of tall grass:
a house of eyes, and in that glistening river
twenty-eight young men are soaping up –
four more than our two dozen.

Then think of fingers working in a solitary room,
working hard at nothing.
That's what all this
saltwater harvest
comes to:
a slippery subject.

i. *Safe*

Can you can you can you tell
how the oyster makes his shell?

His hermetically sealed clean-room?
Studded with barnacles – doubly armoured –
he's made himself a case for his problems:

less a burn-bag than a portable safe
pulled from the wreckage of a sea-crash –
a safe, or a charred steel briefcase.

Customs would like to know the contents.
Let's check the manifest, if it's not ashes.

Item: the grey posset and curd
of a brain for transplant.

The case is still locked, miraculously enough,
and still chained to appetite's half-melted handcuff.

ii. *Surrender*

To the oyster, it's an open-and-shut case, until:
his roots are wrenched up. Tin bucket. Wire brush.
Then a shucking knife like a sword-stub,
after a lifetime's stropping at desire –
a small blade, but enough.

It works at him
till he's snipped,
sloshed loose in the coffin
which he'd clung to so tightly,
to which he'd so tightly clung,

the coffin of his home,
his castle, his keep, his Martello tower,
his Maginot Line bunker,
the masonry of his former might,
blind walls that bound him blindly.

Not long after, at the prodding
of some tiny devil's pitchfork
or the raw suction of some Gargantua's lungs
his salt-thick, speechless tongue
lies on a hot pink tongue.

iii. *Prophecy*

And when you slit that muscle
the oyster gives it up:
gives up its secrets, its disembodied brain or heart
suspended in a brine of life-support,

motionless but alive,
the hinge on which its whole world hinges, snapped.
For the hungry shucker,
there's always that second of thrill,

excitement in black-and-white,
as she comes eye to eye
with the ocean's ancient eye,
so long squeezed shut:

the oyster a shrunken prophetess
spooned into a stone amphora
that some king in a fit of pique
corked up and blipped

into fifty meters
of blue-black sea off Naxos
to lay down the nacreous lamellae
of her death-wish.

This eye that's starved
to make a prophecy –
this eye that's just caught sight of you.
It has so much to say.

11.

If I fasted and wept
for forty days and nights

over the bare moon
of this white plate

a dozen on the half-shell
is all I'd get;

not one more oyster –
not even that.

I weep for the world
with oyster tears,

and 'deeply sympathize',
my heart hardening

under the world's hard gaze
to a grey bolus, more cherrystone

than chowder-sized –
and you'll buy these lies

I'm serving, just as I'll buy yours.
Because who can weep

for forty days and nights?
And who believes that holy stones

for all their worth and weight
never exaggerate?

12.

i. *The Reckoning*

The meal's long done – we et 'em all,
though neither of the two of us
is ready yet
to foot the bill.

Our server brings more finger-bowls
while out back through the swinging doors
a busboy in a pristine smock and hat
is sprinkling sawdust on an ugly spill.

Calcium carbonate and ice,
ice and calcium carbonate
are all that's left on this white plate.
But lover, there's something I forgot to say –

there's something I haven't said
yet. Hidden somewhere in this heap
of broken-backed shells
there's something I forgot –

ii. *Appetite*

will keep on coming. It can't be beat;
in whatever hereafter

we manage to procure, or manufacture,
the flotsam in a bath of bitter tears

is what the children of the Earth
will have to learn to eat:

marine snow, the fraction of bloom and bone
falling like manna on the aphotic zone.

Who'll be the first? Who'll be the bold one?
Size up your daughters and sons.

Tell them we ate the living flesh of sea-hags,
that, like demi-gods, we swallowed the monster's tongue.

Tell them we were Geat-gods, or Poseidons,
that we inhaled matter, pure life-force

to engender our young.
And tell them how wrong

we were; tell them how we're always wrong:
that the seed of the gods that fell into the sea is gone.

Tell them what they'll have to do to survive:
descend to the very bottom of the world,

where the sea-lice and the hagfish writhe
in the hovel of a crushed grey whale,

and fight the ocean itself, the very ocean
for the last of its carrion

in the cold storage unit
of its infinite,

fish-lit morgue;
cannibalize the mummies of Gog and Magog,

the corpse of Sedna, and countless sea-dogs
pickled in airless brine;

comb the tangle of lost dragnets
and nylon lines

for scraps of bait and strangled adolescents,
snip the worms that warm themselves

at sulphurizing vents,
crunch coral like a humphead parrotfish,

and sieve for the spawn of the vampire squid.
Tell them they'll dine on vinegar and bread

and something rooting around in this dark bed
that tastes no different alive or dead.

THE SYCORAX QUIZ

When my body and the twisted tree's are one,
then I'll begin to live my proper lifespan.
       – from Meng Chiao, 'Song of the Old Hills'

Q:

What's Sycorax, who bent over backwards for me –
cirque-du-soleil'd in slo-mo out of *The Matrix*
and rolled back down the page-turn of the century
through Dustbowl streets as a game of hoop-and-stick?

My granddad chased her through the Great Depression,
no belt in his belt-loops but a loop of old rope,
not knowing he was after the Witch, who kept *rollin', rollin'*
into the ecliptic of my mother's hula hoop –

that space-age tube orbiting her waist
like the life-giving rings of the *Maschinenmensch*,
drawn by the gravity well of her serious face –
mother holding her halo in place with a lifelong clench –

till again the Witch flew off, into time's odd angles.
Now I chase her down through dreams, though she makes
       me run,
and I ask myself, which of her games will I tumble
into, when I've chased her back to my generation?

A:

Maybe she's time's arrow – the arrow of thermodynamics,
a trick-shot looping through a shrinking universe;
born from our intuition, but murdered by our facts,
a personification ageing in reverse –

or maybe she's my self-portrait in a chrome sphere
bending over backwards to impress the family dead,
a fish-eyed monster etched by Maurits Escher,
all nose, no head –

but wherever she flees into the curves of space-time,
I know she's spindling me with her sea-cables
to set son against mother, milk the old pantomimes
of blame; she's split a tapped-out sugar maple

where I'll twist myself raw for aeons,
pinned in the splinters of its tuning fork
until a grey shaman pimps his daughters and sons
over the queen's pawn and the king's rook.

Whoever wins, I won't survive the idea
of her, though I'll outlive her. In her son's wild face
I'll glimpse her beauty, but her flexibility
dies with her, her sea-nymph gracefulness:

the way she freefalls backwards, like into a feather-bed
but then catches herself by her own slim heels –
a blue-eyed cipher, ready to roll backwards
to the invention of the zero and the wheel.

LIFE SCIENCES

REVISION

for F. E. R. Simons

i.

The hydra was rearing out of the swamp,
the dwarf paladin was trapped in a man-eating flower,

Theseus was halfway to the minotaur,
and Hannibal was ready to break camp –

but it was all on hold – work before play –
and my homework was never finished until bedtime.

The homework answered to a higher power:
editor, mother, one and the same.

Report or essay or review,
I lost track of the drafts, the endless drafts

I typed and retyped – then the old computer's chime,
the hum of the disk drive, and the printer's chatter

that rewrote what I meant, then what I thought,
then who I was and what I knew.

ii.

Tonight, Theseus would have to freeze,
tracing the labyrinth with the right-hand rule;

the questing dwarves would have to sit tight
on the Hyperborean glacier-ice

as I stared at the paper moths
pressed against the panes of a mid-May night

and rewrote the life of one of the deputies
of the North-West Mounted Police.

For the hundredth time, I heard it save
with the whir of the magnetic drive;

and again the dot-matrix printer gnashed
its pins like a telegram:

not to order me to Shanghai or Assam
but to tell me the revolution was quashed.

iii.

And for the hundredth time I slouched
down the dark, cream-carpeted hall

to the kitchen's accordion door,
then over the kitchen's abattoir tiles

scrubbed so hard, they'd almost been scrubbed out –
to that table under pitiless light,

a table without silverware, a table laid
with books and legal pads, a masquerade

banquet of paper, piled on the 'working cloth'
that after dinner replaced

the linen 'dining cloth',
to hear her chant like a prioress:

The washing-up was my chore,
your chore is to get this right …

iv.

And I'd hand my latest ephemera,
Bellerophon's soon-to-be-slaughtered chimaera,

over to those soft hands and those hard eyes –
uncertain if they shone with love, or wrath –

and I'd stand there, penitent, in her aura
that burned away all superfluities,

all hazy phrase – and left, in their place, prescriptions:
arrows that bled me, but pointed at perfection.

I thank her now, in the end –
not for my fantasies, but for how to mend them –

for the endless raising of that blood-red pen,
for her stern, *I'll read it now – stand there and wait,*

to the inevitable, *No, you don't have it yet –*
write it again.

Threatened by a vortex of wasps,
the glass frog imitates his treasure-troves:
a glar of struggling frogspawn on the cusp
of a leaf-spear. Don't suppose

his transparency, his invisibility's
any kind of cowardice.
His *ushiro-geri* – his back kick – is as deadly
as a martial artist's: a slick air-slice

like the chameleon's
plunger-tipped tongue,
a wet-coiled weapon
wound and sprung, wound and sprung,

smother-smashing wasp-wing gossamer.
Many rely on him.
He will be mother.
His organs swim

like an amoeba's organelles
in the vessel of himself.
His pulse is a liquid crystal
shimmer of self-belief.

He has nothing to hide
but his thoughts. Tormented by wasps,
he and I elide
their buzzing. With one prehensile foot, I'll grasp

the poison thorn
of each wasp-sting –
drown the drone
of their endless concurring –

and with the other, cling
to nature – to one green spear,
cradle to these unborn offspring:
these tadpoles, these struggling tears.

HERMIT CRABS

The hermits have pluralized
in this nook of a Burmese beach,
wedding-white as Crab Key –
a swap meet for the Hermit Outreach
Hotline, or a hermit key party

on occupied real estate:
smack in the white-hot cleavage
of coral dunes – a talcummed shimmy
on powdered sea-finery,
as if Poseidon's do-no-wrong blanched bull

were left alone to do his worst
with the Minoan earthenware
for a thousand years –
or left to tread whole grape-harvests
to the purple tincture of this farther coast.

The hermits scrabble
for a score at any price –
getting it on, right out
in the open: an impromptu
neighbourhood orgy,

a joust of houseboats
and mobile homes,
titillation at full tilt
in the voyeur-stare of the sun.
The sand whispers *Make a wish*

and *Since we'll never see each other again...*
and the waves say, *Shhhhh, baby, shhhhh.*
I stand and watch for a while.
Then I add an empty shell –
something like a 'spotted unicorn' –

to the knocking pile,
and wonder which hornèd couple or triple
will be the first to notice
they're locked in a love-scrum
with a simulacrum,

with a cowrie's porcelain kiss:
that the next-door neighbour's gone,
that no shell can make room for two,
that every love-nest's a coffin
vacated by its architect,

that every occupation's just a squat,
that every nest is empty
from the moment of its secretion
to the moment we're told to pack –
and we carry the rooms we mate in on our backs.

There are so many to choose from
but we are not one of them.

Not that we needed to go underground –
not that our love was in any way illicit
but we treated it like it was: hell-bent, hell-bound,
as if we were complicit
in some fatal plan or conspiracy:
a love like a pair of nuclear weapon keys.

We went underground, literally.
We made love in the kind of darkness that sticks:
not the fake dark of a bedroom with drawn blinds
but the dark of abandoned fall-out shelters and mines,
where we laid the plans for our own facility,
a maze to confuse superficial semantics.

Maybe it was the Cold War 'Diefenbunker'
in the Ottawa suburbs – that worst-case scenario
turned tourist attraction, that atomic elf-barrow,
where I first kissed you from suburbs to epicentre,
deep in a man-made karst: a teenage conspiracy theorist
making love to a debunker.

Years later, maybe it was one of the few crypts
worthy of our worship – the crypt of the House of Commons –
where I lay my suit coat under your bottom,
where I lay my head on the cold flagstones
under the shaft and flanges of a mace: my brain, my bones
feeling a new facility, under sentence of your lips.

Decades later, it must have been Postojna's caves,
where a train runs through a ballroom white as salt – a
          chandeliered ballroom –
where I led you astray like false fire, like a glow-worm,

into a side-tunnel, and your cold fingers slipped home
dextrously as a blindworm, as an olm,
to rub light into life, from ember to blaze.

Wherever this facility of ours was, it drove
my expansion plans, my plans for a whole new level
beyond the cave-blindness of adolescence –
to build a complex too deep for bunker-busters
or ground-penetrating radar,
a research facility, a site for new developments –

but primarily for refining sex into permanence.
It's no bomb shelter, no Lost World to cope
with this one, but a habitable foundation for hope:
a maze of bioluminescence – a maze that love extends,
where our steps are lit by the decay
of long-dead lovers in their graves.

So no maybes: it was all this interiority –
chamber after chamber of unmaidenly thoughts
and deeds – our deep landscapes of stalagmites,
crevasses, cul-de-sacs, dripping grottoes –
that dug us in, that mapped our subterranean
thirst for each other's surfaces and veins.

Whatever it is, whatever it grows, or holds
in store, we grew it together, this facility,
the way the earth secretes its rarest crystals:
atoms at a time, not for commercial sale,
not for industry – the way soil germinates seeds
well out of sight, in warmth the world thinks cold.

FLAVA

after Spenser, *Amoretti*, Sonnet 37

Her hair, that hair! – that swish, that golden style
 she's got from some hairapist-to-the-stars –
 I'm fine if it's a weave, a Golden Mile
 of extensions: hair like that makes love go far.
Is it just me, obsessing with her hair?
 Or does this siren tangle everyone
 with tresses like that – twist them like steel rebar
 torn up by her blow-dryer's hot typhoon?
Be cool – keep it together – flirting's fun
 until it all turns real. Enjoy it while
 that golden lasso hasn't leashed you. Once
 she lands her noose, you'll strangle with a smile:
that hair will be your chains, your cuffs, your collar –
the net that fishes you, old gladiator.

TREE SNAKE

How could I regret your precedent –
time's murder of variety –
as I stand eyeing your jewelled recompense,
a green-bronze pendant in a tinted case,

coil heaped on coil, the throne made of the tyrant,
the tyrant queen recumbering, seemingly
sleepy-eyed, but torsion-tense,
the spring behind the clock-face?

Lumbering, mud-bellied reptiles came and went
while you refined yourself to be
linear as text – as great events
are inked, engraved, then later, traced –

then scrawled on blackboards, each smudged testament
shedding the skins of its complexity –
as your ecdysial brilles cement
from diamond brilliants to paste,

clouding your iris-slits with discontent
at the weight of whispered history –
late libels on your innocence
when you slid past our garden-gates,

pasquils your paved skin rebuffs, reinvents
with stereoscopic clarity –
this reptile house held in suspense,
the contents of your tank steam-blurred, a no-place,

a world of mist and phosphorescence
wreathing your tree-throne's canopy,
a glassed-in oracle where supplicants
itching to shed their surfaces

stand still, snake-stopped, and learn to circumvent
vestigial complexities:
identity in fingerprints,
all passing claims to species, gender, race –

hypnotised by your pseudo-monument:
your silence, coiled in mastery
of the radius of your striking distance
from the knowledge, and the tree.

TWO POEMS FOR ELINOR

1. *Charms*

Between the geometries she taught me
of orthogonal and parallel,
the use of the right triangle
for the right job, the use of the unit circle,
Elinor clipped other keys

to the key-ring of my survival –
Elinor one year older than my
ten-year-old summer luxury
that any learning could be put by
until the first leaves fell.

She taught me, for example, that wishes
have magnitude and weight:
that if you time it right
you can accumulate
infinite fortune and riches

by degrees – so kiss red when you see
11:11 on the clock;
strategize every wishbone-break;
wish on fallen eyelashes, wish on your birthday cake;
look sharp and you can stockpile divinity,

your karma trickle-charging your desires.
Later on from other girls
came superstitions I found more useful:
a necklace of soda-can ring-pulls;
plucking daisies; leaping over campfires;

locking pinkies while locking eyes;
and how, whispered into a well,
a night-wish could catch an angel
better than a churchyard bell,
or a wish whispered at sunrise

could shiver an ear's pink seashell –
but the mane of the dandelion
and brown pennies thrown in a fountain
and catching mid-air the fallen
helicopters of the maple

remained Elinor's discrete domain –
as, through years less fortunate,
wishing on a meteorite's
incision in a summer night
remained mine.

Our mother favoured charms to ward off fault:
a life without ladders
or breakable mirrors.
Over her shoulder
pinch after pinch of salt.

2. *Cereal*

By the rushlight of *Spider-Man* reruns
on our black-and-white Viking,
by the foxlight of an Atari commercial
my ten-year-old heart obeyed its festival.

Saturday morning and frosted cereal,
cross-legged in front of the telly: a ritual
in every house in suburbia but ours –
and so my secret covenant, my lost hours.

Upstairs, in surgical gloves and apron,
clashing through the cutlery drawers,
wearing earplugs and hollering for my sister,
my mother was desperate for something.

She seemed to be feeling rather set-upon.
Through her stoppered ears,
above her ruckus and her summoning wail –
the racket of her weekly Reformation –

she could still somehow glean
the chime of a pagan prayer-bell:
my spoon against the bottom of my bowl.
I froze like a prairie dog trapped between

flood and fire at the two mouths of his bolt-hole.
I held the volume's variable resistor
a breath from mute, as bell-jarred Mysterio
coalesced in a puff of what had to be indigo.

Then I jerked in fright.
My fingers slipped on the rheostat
as Elly's corn-yellow braids condensed
out of the dark beside me, in the glare

of my desaturated heroes and villains,
her little whisper tense.
'There's going to be a cull,' she warned,
and checked a bowl was clean.

I passed her a fresh box
of Honey-Nut Something
or *Oh, Dem Golden Grahams.*
She went up to her elbow

in the sugared pumice
and dredged the free toy
up to the cereal-surface:
Captain Nemo's bicarbonate-

of-soda-powered *Nautilus.*
Up in the kitchen our mother had ceased to bray.
We watched as Peter Parker exchanged a chaste
embrace with Mary Jane –

her grey hair, I knew, really fox-flame.
In my bowl, my milk and sugared wheat
had made a sort of paste.
Wearing a cling-film face pack, mother tiptoed

down the back stairs, bearing, I imagined,
what surely must have been a burning brand,
and humming a Sunday hymn a day too soon.
I took my sister's hand.

THE CERES OF SUBURBIA

'No more a virgin, gone the garish meadow...'
– Louis MacNeice

This new-sprawl, big-box prairie mall
where my daughter works an evening shift
is a neon cornucopia:

titanic quince and pomegranates,
persimmons, purple plums, and dates
under the pregnant prairie clouds –

and often, in my nightmares now,
under the blanket of the snow,
the killing blanket of the snow –

although my daughter's never seen
one winter, even at thirteen,
one snowflake more than what her mirror

reflects of teenage beauty's hex.
Past the mall parking lot, the dark
slides its hand all the way up

the Arctic Circle's shivering thigh:
first over scrubland, and the throb
of diggers and high-tension lines –

another suburb taking shape,
communities with walls and gates –
and on, past these, the farm-scape –

the soil soft as my daughter's breath
under its quilt of wheat and rape.
But always through the night I hear

down the highway's tarmac-snakes
the war-drums of the lost boys' bikes.
And so: each night I drop her off

and pick her up, give her a lift
home to a table set for two,
cereal and milk – the snack she likes –

home to mum – the former farmer's wife,
figuring – fussing – sharp – spendthrift –
and frayed, tuned to the smallest sign

of her only daughter's seasonal drift.
But we're not there, we're not there yet –
with miles to go before that table's set.

I browse and watch till closing time:
her forehead's furrow as she does the maths,
figuring her gains, her hourly worth,

throwing shy smiles at seasonal mates.
Then she scans 'No Sale' – closes the till –
shrugs off her apron's olive-drab –

pops the top button on her blouse –
and all through this I watch and browse.
They see us, the Plutonians –

I feel their spider-eyes stare up
from underground, from basalt caverns –
unblinking eyes like poison-pips.

Now comes the moment when it counts
to have me as her chaperone,
to take her, will she, nill she, home:

she punches her card, they kill the lights.
Between mall-neon and the ice-white glare
of my station wagon's headlamps

she shakes off my hand as we bridge the night:
Mum, I'm fine – my mates will see –
Six paces, four – my stomach cramps.

But I beat them, still. I beat the odds –
the trace and champ of bored-stiff gods.
And so what, if she slumps on her bed

untouched, unmanned, and still unnamed,
alive to nothing but her dreams
of pale, androgynous metal gods?

I'll kill to keep her as long as I can –
sullen – barren – feckless – blithe –
here on the surface, here with me,

in the fallow field of her untilled sense
while I stave off winter, and we both thrive,
stumping the Underlord's tumescence

like a giant, misshapen sugar beet
buckling the tarmacked-over soil
of the parking lot under my daughter's feet.

MOLE

The mole points a finger
that comes straight to the point,
the point of his resolve:
that stone-tooled, time-tooled awl.

He's come up to work
in rural St Norbert, breast-stroking
through soil's starless waters,
evading the barrage lines

with bank and barrel-roll:
the draped mist-nets
of willow- and weed-roots –
buffing a rhizome

with a felt shoulder.
All earth's his tome
to fumble through
with those scholar-lily hands

branked in miner's gauntlets.
He'd throw them down, but can't.
Buried up to his neck
in the sweet black,

he wants the soil even higher –
drags the turf-covers
up over his head
to hide his night-labours

from the prairie stars.
His forbearers
rubbed down the spirals
of their ears to escape

the parish's waking bell
and the bell for sleep –
purged the images of day
and the twilight's revelries

till both were dim enough
for the half-moons
of his *pince-nez*.
He snuffles back down

his long tunnel
to Dulce Domum.
With his twin trowels
he knocks night-clots

from the soles
of his pink Wellies,
then heads for the pantry.
As if a plough or a guillotine

shared one fate between us,
he's become my totem,
my soft little moan.
His half's to potter alone –

to sweep and shine
the forked roots
of mossy molars –
the parish headstones –

with the chamois of his swim.
My half's to follow him:
to polish myself down to moleskin,
to crawl down that tunnel

and meet him where he's curled
in his garden-variety Underworld;
to join him in his pantry
and share a nibble,

and speak of the artistry
of his withdrawal;
to learn how he's made his solitude
palatable.

Down one of his garden-tunnels
that runs all the way to Selkirk,
I hear the two of us in conference,
starting the spadework.

First a voice – my childhood voice,
that first little moan of despair.
Then his whispered reply,
after what seems like years:

Now we are getting somewhere.

NOJIRI HOPPER

Lake Nojiri, Nagano Prefecture

In a vertical angle
of my cabin's ramshackle

plywood and water-damage moiré
this Nojiri hopper's splayed

a textbook landing
on one blackened gas-ring

above the enamelled Mare Imbrium
of my moon-cratered oven.

He's the perfect landing-craft for Io, or Titan:
six legs, planted hexagon,

under a carapace of gold mylar
to scatter the solar flares.

I half-expect him to separate
into two parts – *mission complete* –

sending his head and thorax
pluming on ion rockets

back up through the gravity well
to some sleeping command module.

His curling antennae,
half again as long as his whole body

quiver and twitch their signal link
all the way back to Jodrell Bank.

He's all delicate equipage –
delicate but space-age.

I lean in for a closer look.
He doesn't budge at the chinook

of my breath, my sudden atmosphere.
He's conserving every ampere

for the return flight.
How far's he come, this summer night,

arcing between these summer stars,
these satellite-winks, these meteor-showers?

What far Cape or Cosmodrome
has he launched from?

He'll scan me and I'll scan him
till he hurls himself at his next whim,

unless this salt-plain of white enamel
and scorched metal

is a survey-zone for his colony
of willing exiles, giving up the city,

turning their backs on the iniquity
of the hive, the cells of Babylon;

or unless he's a colony of one,
like me, among Nojiri's Christian missionaries,

a heretic of Nojiri-ko
in a controlled descent

from an old Apollo –
a pagan, but always ready to repent.

HAIKU

summer moon –
I've lost everything
unnecessary

They've levelled a square
block by my work – I can see
what was always there.

a thousand gold fans,
a thousand green: two factions
fight for one *ginnan*

outside the station
shiitake sprang up last night:
these broad-brimmed pilgrims

this old abacus
floating with the bladderwrack:
teeth of the Heike

I limp up the hill:
my old bad leg's now become
the best of the two.

a dying beetle –
indistinguishable from
a dead leaf's scuttle

those silver *saba*
ranged on ice in the market:
this smiling air crew

I drain my glass:
cold *nihon-shu* in Gunma.
The caged bear shivers.

LELANTOS THE HUNTER

(a song from Old Llyr)

Though I carried an axe with two crescent blades –
the moon in the pool above the weir –
though I carried a quiver with twelve barbed points,
and a horn-bow, and a boar-spear,

the stars I followed, tracking your spoor
for your priceless pelt – its dappled weight –
pricked out Actaeon's demise
and tireless Orion's tiresome fate –

so I built my blind at your favourite pool
and nocked an arrow, and bent the bow,
watching you lap, but I never loosed –
and all this happened long ago –

the way our hunts live on in the stars,
after the fact, to fool the next
hunter, or prey, who reads their lore:
Look, there's Lelantos – he expects

things to go badly from the start
when he does what he was born to do:
scared of the catch in a cursed art,
playing, but never playing through –

aiming a little off the mark
so whenever he misses, he can claim
it was just an untipped shaft, for practice,
or that every hunt's a game.

He jerks at flash-pops on the evening news.
Dreams of the speed-bag pacemaker his pulse.

Slumped in his corner, he can't hear his muse,
a ring-girl smiling past the bells, the catcalls:

in heels and rhinestone swimsuit, she's endured
worse than men's leers, to lift her numbered placard.

Three minutes at a go, he'll talk ten rounds
arguing there's drama in the ropes, the ring –

tell you how he drew, but never once went down –
writing in prose, at least, spares him the counting.

By day his ham-fist cramps around his pen
or hangs there, slack, while he talks man-to-man.

He dreams of weeping in the arms of men
and being beaten with a frying pan.

THE KUNG FU MASTER'S RÉSUMÉ

The kung fu master looked over his résumé:
his start-up had just gone belly-up or
face-down on a thousand pounds of new practice mats;
the lines of credit were cut; the staff in an uproar –

hadn't they heard there's a recession on?
But you have to look out for number one,
and he was the entrepreneur: 'Death Fist, Inc.'
was his baby. The fun was over, but it *had* been fun,

and he'd keep his head up, while all the others sank.
So what's next for the boss, the *sifu*, the *sensei*,
now that he's packed up his swords and his sparring pads
and pulled down the poster advising, 'Preparation is the Best
    Defence'?

He sat in his office one last time,
eyeing the heaped corpses of the company accounts,
and read through his résumé, weighing his options,
trying not to think about which of his cheques would bounce.

It was a brilliant résumé, but would they believe it?
Or would they find his achievements a touch – abstract?
Created a workforce of invulnerable men and women –
Remodelled head office to withstand ninja attacks –

And what about his skill set? Did it lack relevance?
Can punch through a block of reinforced concrete –
Can turn the strength of multiple opponents against them –
Can stand on his hands and fight with his feet –

Would they say he needed to 'diversify his experience'?
No, he'd read *Fortune* magazine – his skills would impress them.
Shows no mercy in competition – every CEO had that one,
the same goes for *Trains employees to obey without question.*

Some doubts circled like assassins, but he fought them off,
like the nightmare of the only interview question he dreaded:
'What is it you can actually *do*?' In dreams, he gives the honest
    answer:
I can get away from anyone – and then hit them bloody hard.

He had a degree in physics – once thought he'd go into finance –
or something to do with computers – something profitable.
But a hobby became a career: the sweat-stink, the locked gazes,
and the thrill of the thud as someone else took the fall.

THE TAI QI STUDENT

for Col Maggs

He wishes as he winds through
pre-occupied empty space

that he could leave some trail
from every limb, some trace

to hold these curves just so,
to map his loops in the air,

some track of his path and progress
through the art of self-awareness –

so he might know, at last,
where those who have gone before him

have gone – become pure movement,
or fallen, like silent snow –

and, like a Zen garden pebble
or a shark-white go stone

his next move might unfold
as *being*, not as *doing*,

but not being here, but *there*,
not here touching the air like a test –

like a test, but in reverse,
questions following answers,

impulse following force –
as he asks with his whole body,

with knees, and elbows, and hips,
with flowing hands and wrists:

is this the path, or the forest?
and this? and this? and this?

YŌKAI: AKANAME ('FILTH LICKER')

i.

Sooner or later,
we all have a run-in with the filth licker –

furred flesh-snacker,
grubbing tongue like a cheese grater,

lobeless earholes cocked at the water-rush
of bath-plash and toilet flush –

ghoul of our urban sprawl,
haunter of public pools and sewer tunnels.

From the Yoshiwara soaplands to Chiyoda's
sentōs and spas

he plays cattle-bird and bluestreak wrasse
to the slack-jawed shoals of the working classes.

He lives on human *aka* –
the dead skin-flakes of scrubbing brush and loofah –

hopping in the dark like a man-shaped toad,
his thousand pink mouth-tendrils disembogued

around an intestinal hoover-snout.
He's a sommelier of vintage grout,

flatulenting at cracked plastic and porcelain,
slobbering right up under the rim.

ii.

I hadn't scrubbed the splash-room since forever –
and when did I last mop the kitchen floor?

When I stumbled down at three in my garish
pyjamas, for the weary week-night slash

I jumped at the shadow
hunched by the *o-furo* –

in no wise a water-nymph or a woodwose,
since I'm standing there half-asleep in Tokyo's

evergrey labyrinth of concrete fens
where the suitblacked and bootblacked salarymen

cross the five rivers
for fifty years

zombying their days out in honourable despair
without ever thinking a single river was there.

I thought maybe a *tanuki* – a raccoon-pup –
had clambered up the drainpipe.

But I hadn't heard a sound.
Spring mould had turned the taps and drains rust-brown –

watabokori hid under the sliding doors.
The bleach-smell of the blooming azaleas

lurked like a starched night nurse
snoozing upright in purple curlers

in the lane behind the house.
That smell must have driven the lickers to despair:

down to the sewers – or in this case,
indoors, to risk a face-to-face

run-in with a human host.
His good luck to get a bachelor – a filth licker pig-roast.

We sized each other up like two sick men
studying their innards on a CT scan.

I moved to close the door to keep it at bay,
and it said '*Matte-kure* –

nisshukan de shokuji wo shitemasen.' So it speaks
modern Japanese. Is polite. And hasn't eaten in weeks.

Poor toad, poor spit-faced mess –
the housewives around here are meticulous.

iii.

The filth licker can pinpoint a dirty bog
from miles away, even through city smog,

through Shibuya's perfume counters and city drains,
and the stronger stenches of the fast food chains.

I guess I had what he needed, and our mutualism
meant I'd get a grooming – a spritzing

and a spotless tub. But like a marine zoologist, I knew
these cleaners take more than your parasites and mildew –

you tip them with a bit of muscle and mucus membrane,
the way most of nature's exchanges

involve some blood, some pain – even when it's complicit.
But I closed my eyes and told him to have at it –

I couldn't bear to see a living thing
come over to mine for dinner and leave starving.

His blade-furred tongues shaved my head and beard
closer than Vidal Sassoon's scissors could,

cleaned my ears without trimming the lobes –
then gave me a full-body exfoliating rub

that left me sleepy-soft and baby-pink.
I left him doing my *isu, oke,* and sink

and staggered back upstairs
for three more blissful hours.

When the cicadas revved me out of my dreams
I washed again, blinded by the bathtub's gleam

in the dawn-sun,
feeling like I'd spent the night at a pricey *onsen.*

My filth licker had slouched away,
back down to his mouldy den,

and left me as clean as if I'd been autoclaved,
hoping to see him again.

THE STENT

Yon king's to me like to my father's picture
Telling me in its glory what he was...
Where now his son's a glow-worm in the night,
That makes its fire from darkness, not from light;
Whereby I see that time's the king of men:
He's both their parent and their grave,
Giving them what he will, not what they crave.

I

They pushed the stent into my father's arm
like some blood-amulet, some ancient charm.
Hearing him tell it from across an ocean
as I lay beside my sleeping new-born son,
I felt the ghost of a flutter in my chest
like an echo of his cardiac arrest,
followed by a wave of abject gratitude,
my thankfulness that such a magnitude
of expertise exists in medicine
to pull us back to being, from being a has-been.
No mountebank's trick, no faith-healer's scams:
they pushed it up through veins, red cells, and plasma,
an old man's matter – matter of man and boy,
his blood acclimatizing to its alloy;
a lease on life few men could deserve more
since he gave his whole life to prove what cures,
and what's just rosewater and sugar-pill:
the careful measure of our miracles
by a high priest of Aesculapius and Apollo,
a hierophant of the pharmacological.

This tribute to my father, my self's starter,
starts when he's eight: pharmacy's acolyte
cycling through Bristol's shattered stained-glass light,
a choir boy with no more church to serve in
now that the City of Churches was in ruins.
He did the round with his deliveries,
pedalling through the lanes of Nether Stowey
with a basketful of analgesia:
the chemist's boy, passing the pier at Clevedon
and the big house where they grew the penicillin.
So now, the miracle's recipient,
he's paid back with a smidge – a jewel of talent
blooming to stretch the *tunica media*
of a coronary artery, somewhere –
a system retrofit after a scare.
The stent expands my father's flesh, and days,
lets him live on, outpacing death's pursuit
to read, at last, this long-overdue praise
from a son who'd call him wiser than Cnut.
The stent can stretch the days of anyone
not quite ready for oblivion –
can hold the line for anyone not ready
for death – and who's ready? Who has said: '*Me* –
come on – let's do it now'? And who'd want such
a dead-eyed ringer joining life's fixed match?
And so: the open gowns, the care that hurts,
the surgeries to cut out or to insert
flesh, or its reinforcements, bits like stents
that might forestall our sempiternal absence.

The stent's a relic, a bronzed scrap of fishnet
or fishnet stocking won from a coquette,
or a tassle fallen from some Magdalene;
or it's a new design for a siege engine
sketched out in sand or wax by Archimedes,

a worm to undermine our enemies'
petards – or our own hardened arteries.
The stent's both armour – worn internally –
and a core sampler's drill bit that invades
the bloodstream of a willing convalescent,
or it's a palliative shrapnel-fragment,
like 'arrow' in the *kanji* for physician,
like how most cures start with the scalpel blade.
Thanks to it, there's no past I'd rather live in –
pasts without stents or continuity.
A past where he died now makes no sense to me.
Till now I've lived my life out in the Bronze Age,
preferring to 'drill down', to disengage,
to strike out with the antiquarians,
with Dr Syntax and the Casaubons,
to imitate the slowworm and the mole –
fossorial square pegs wedged into round holes.
But it only takes one heart attack, one stent
to sit up, breathless, shocked back to the present.
Father, I'm ready to become the son
that you deserved, who's outlived his assumption
he'd always be a boy, and not a man.
I'll trim the wastage from my surplus lifespan.
We try to cheat death's cold clinch every day,
and when I go, I'm going the same way:
biting, low-kicking, aiming for death's crotch.
Father, your masked and mid-life champion
has come, to idealize you as someone
who looks at death the way he checks his watch –
glancingly, someone just being accurate
when calculating how much time they've got;
even though now I know you're just like me,
terrified of your own mortality.
To be a man is learning how to hide it:
to feel death's sucker-punch, to take that hit

square in the chest; and, trying not to freeze,
get on with paying the utilities.

2

They patched him up, life's cotton-masked enforcers,
the rubber-gloved and pink-gowned choristers
of a Bosch or Bacon *Hallelujah* mass –
mute shadows of our first empiricists.
The halogen-haloed angels of the cath lab,
nameless to me, returned him stitched, gift-wrapped,
stretching our love-quotient a little further
by dealing more days to a gentle father.
A father much like the heart in question here,
a heart good for a hundred metaphors:
for instance, how the myocardium
that feeds the heart is such a selfless system,
arteries sipping at what blood they can
from the mainstream – the systemic circulation
powering the arms and legs, the brains and guts –
not stinting them when there's a power cut
but stiffening, gradually sipping less and less,
taking the strains of crisis and stenosis
till arms and legs and guts drive the old horse
past all endurance, hauling the cart (or hearse)
of body mass till pain hammers the bell,
purpling the lips that mouthed *I look quite well
for my age.* Well. Well, it's just one example –
one fitful squeeze of the left ventricle –
one of a hundred metaphors for a heart
whose actual vessels show where the man starts –
or few men worth the name, but him for certain.

Where was I? Where *was* I? They put the stent in,
with me not even there to hold the hand
that held my own, when I could barely stand
on crutches, with a broken knee or ankle –
assayed and fractured in the crucible
of district or provincial junior heats,
or shaking with the exhaustion of defeat
after a hard fall on the judo mats,
their sweet *tatami* scent drowned in old sweat,
my *judo-gi*, Lavinia's robes ripped open,
speechless and sick from the adrenaline,
pale from the bruising and the choke-chafed throat,
and from the judo-mums' bloodthirsty shouts:
there was his hand, his heart, to brush it off,
not to say *Tough it out* just to look tough,
but to toughen me in the vice of his embrace:
the white-hot furnace of the alchemist
or swordsmith folding steel under his hammer,
folded and worked, ten thousand times, the heat
not faltering, the rhythm not missing a beat,
hammering out the blade and the blade's burr,
shaping the *shigane* and *hagane*
as if my bloodless face were the steel's grey,
his love forging a carbon-steel sword
sharp enough to slice the proverbial silk cord
without fraying a thread, a legendary
sword like the *Kusanagi-no-Tsurugi*,
a two-edged blade – not *katana*, but *ken*,
that will not break, but flexes as it bends:
the tense-potential man, the fathered state,
the future tense no loss can abrogate –
a state of mind no hate, no lictor's lashes,
no factory line, no Communist or Fascist

reel of the mob, no cog, no oligarchy,
no hothouse atmosphere or rising sea,
no herd mentality, no dirt, no buzz,
no blanketing ash or ignorance of what was
can ever wreck, or rotten state unseat.
It is, perhaps, a love I can't repeat.

4

But when it comes my turn to bare an arm
to 'receive treatment', as they say, to take
my medicine, to undo the mistakes
of chance or willpower, to deflect alarm –
I'll roll my sleeve up, show the spots and scars
that decades and poor judgment helped me gather:
a parchment-pale old arm, its power dilute.
And I'll take the odds, finding them much improved
thanks to what people like my father made
on arse-eroding lab stools, spectrum-eyed,
plying the sceptic's plectrum – the pipette.
It cost him so much that I hope he'd say
he still believes that no one else should pay
for their DNA's instabilities,
for the right to live with health and dignity:
that some costs aren't costs, and some debts aren't debts;
that some investments could have infinite
return, if we could measure living profit,
the pleasure and peace of mind of being whole –
whole societies, whole individuals
set free at last from that primeval cry:
Who'll pay the bills if I get ill, or die?
When there are no more special queues for kings
or corporate pirates and their harpy hirelings,
everyone will receive their medicine –

the stent, the chemo, or the stapled stomach,
the transplant or the anti-psychotics –
the 'thin win', i.e., physical salvation.
Testing their cures, my father may resent
those gifted with the transplant or the stent
who seem unworthy of their miracles,
who'll never change, who'll never break their spirals
of their dependencies on drink, or pills,
or ignorance's echo in their skulls.
He was always more conservative than me:
the dark side of a Salvation Army family
whose doctrine of strict Christian compassion
falls prey to pride, and to the logic-schism
of bootstrap aphorisms: *God helps those*
who help themselves, but Christ, God also knows
some are just on the make – want a free ride –
as if the elites, strutting at being self-made
(so they'd say) don't thrust self-legitimated
fingers into the sweatshop-sewn, sweat-ratted
pockets of the minimum-wage rate-payers,
pockets that have long since begun to fray.

But that's where I come in: the prodigal,
the son who took his privilege to hell
and offered it to Proserpine, in trade for
the time and energy for this strange labour,
whose work (well, not my *work*, as such, but this
underworld gig, hard labour's nemesis)
is mediating generative anger
between the ungrateful children and the father,
whether it's the old father-God – or mine,
a gentleman among barbarians –
or a blind father stumbling towards a cliff,
tricked back to life by a lost son's 'what if'.
The prodigal can mediate between

work ethics, social classes, all extremes,
can show the structures of society
still parallel the systems of the body.
So: I'll speak for the red cells of the stews,
play psychopomp to all the system's losers,
the Falstaffs of the underground flesh-pots –
the alleys stented open like blood-spigots
that keep the crotch as limber as the brain,
that make us come, then send us home again.
I'll speak for the dens of misery and sin
or things that we called sin to rein them in
before we could explain why they might be
more like metaphysical pharmacy,
a panacea in the skimpy dress
of global culture's collective success:
the smoke and white noise of pachinko parlours;
the *film noir* nympholepsy of the bars
where hosts and hostesses get paid to fill
voids of neglect or loneliness until
last call, when the unsubsidized
doses of highballs and lascivious eyes
are tallied and fall due. Or there's the rub
of the massage parlour, or the strip club:
the touch that's paid for, or a whispered extra,
a shadowy exchange rate that neglects the
heart, that rubs scented oil into its symptoms,
markets placebos to love's self-made victims
and their victims, who smear concealer on
their stamps as low-denomination coin,
smiling around their bruises, their self-hate.
The prodigal will offer to translate.
The prodigal carries his father's science
as gratitude, and as his self-defence:
ready to praise the signal and the noise,
ready to argue the pole dancer's poise

is an effect of vaunting, abstract thought;
that our creative powers must find their output
in wasteful pleasures: that at last, catharsis
is heat; that brains must breathe; that the sharp lines
of science and culture flow from endocrines,
that Donne and Einstein stared at their wives' arses.

5

Thanking Aesculapius for my father, I'll
thank my father for living for the mortals:
for living for the work, for measuring
himself against himself, immune to the stings
of fad and fashion, or ambition's needles,
or the lure of the multinationals –
Big Pharma beckoning from across the border,
vamping the siren-song of its disorders,
its stitched-cadaver map of aches and hurts
inflamed by hypochondriacal adverts,
the forty-ninth parallel's gravity well
that every pharmacologist could smell
strong as ammonia, as iron sulphide –
come and be rich – and being rich, dignified –
that every former white-jacketed chemist
could feel, hard as the pestle in his fist:
the offer of too-good-to-be-true lifestyles
my father must have felt – that we all feel.

Writing for him, I'll write what he can't praise,
the motivation for my own late days
that are still, thank God, my father's days: delight
in debunked myths – Bigfoot, the School of Night,
Spring-Heeled Jack, tales of alien abductees –
my delight in stirring up conspiracies

because they make good stories. And delight
in all our wild emotions: this despite
the sense – learned from a father's good example –
that a cool head will let a fracas cool
when voices rise, and tempers start to fray –
empiricism's levee against Doomsday.
What can I say? I like the heat, the fight,
that spike in my blood pressure, and I rate
well-scripted if improbable theatrics
over the modern novel, the *deus ex*
machina over the antithetical
painstaking, patient, analytical
seeping of the gas chromatograph;
I'll gun for drama, for the easy laugh,
the reaching rhyme, the tried-and-tested climax.

At least he taught me how to check my facts,
myth's precursors – their elements and compounds –
fine-tuned to nature's microscopic bounds:
the capillary action of plant fibres,
the reaching and encroaching of amoebas,
the tumble of red blood cells and leukocytes,
the Zen gardens of powdered magnetite:
everything a low-powered microscope
could show a curious child of nature's footnotes,
the fine components of its clouds and trees
and the slow breath of its geologies.
He showed me nature caught between glass slides,
but also, nature as it's crystallised
by literature, transmuted into lines
that remake nature in their verbal confines:
the flowers guarded by Titania's fairies,
the *anthropophagi* of the bestiaries,
the herbs and simples of the nymphs and shepherds,
the hebenon that poisons us with words,

the ruined chantries, and before them, Arthur's
last days, and Lancelot's, days when the wounds
of knights in mortal combat seemed to shed
two or three times the blood they should have had –
as if their valour doubled their blood volumes.
He made science a fit subject for verse;
he made his methods worth writing about;
he taught me secrets that have come to this:
a life devoted to science not in practice,
but in the practice of my faith in doubt.

6

So my days stand on words, words that are bent
on being as clear in their sound-teguments
as those glass sample slides he made for me
to drop a frame around my fantasy,
to lower the lens of an inductive proof
over a flaming Ming Dynasty *qilin*
to turn it back into a sad giraffe.
His garden was the real, and the imagined:
he quantified them, but he didn't judge them.
Cells, animalcules, tardigrades or golems –
he let me make of life what I would make.
So here I am, the sum of my mistakes
and crossings-out, a grown man in rhyme's nursery,
caught by the spell's curse, by sound's cursory
connections to an object's history,
its sustained superficiality.
I'm stained with ink and crystal violet –
the eternal dilettante full of regret,
trying to say something, *anything*, distinct,
amassing trivia as I lip sync
the words of better poets as my own,

the thoughts of better scientists, who've shown
we can rebuild ourselves, can introduce
metal into our organs, can seduce
rational thinking with its own achievements:
can set an alloy mesh like a sea-fence
against indulgence; alloy that allows me
to persist in folly, to asseverate
utility in my dream-chemistries
that let me go on even now, so late,
being a child who can still ring his father,
let me go on being a child outright,
raising galvanic monsters in a brain
he never tried to wire to be a scholar's,
but somehow did – a course I'll set to rights
by promising now to work as I've been trained:
to give up on self-pitying regrets
at making a poor scientist, and bet
on being a fantasist wholeheartedly;
populate my pantheon and bestiary;
stop using science as a spectrometer
to test a line to ten significant digits
but to refine that painstaking skill set
of working harder to be easier,
putting the art of science into art
like this, still harping on my father's heart:
on how the surgery went well, but still,
months afterwards, a cut finger would spill
more blood than Galahad or Percival
had in their veins to give up for the Grail –
how not so much as a hangnail went unstanched,
with his blood full of anticoagulants.

I'll stop trying to impress anyone
and do the work that I consider fun
but no one else enjoys – a definition,

if ever there was one, of true vocation.
I'll let the science guide, and not restrain,
the way a cabinet-maker uses wood-grain:
the line of nature that his plane respects
to shape a box into an artefact
more worthy of the curiosities
it holds – its fossils and automata,
its wind-up scarabs copied from John Dee,
its trigrams and its *tetragrammata*,
its armillary spheres and *netsuke*,
its samples from Tunguska and Pompeii,
its elf-bolts, mermaid-hair, basilisk scales,
relics of gilded teeth and fingernails –
the unreal and the real taxonomies
of its marvellous plant and animal species:
cassia and yarrow, wolfsbane and mandrake;
unicorn horns (both genuine and fake);
stingers and fangs from various manticores;
and smaller marvels, bronzed by myth and lore
to outlast empires, to slink through fire and slander:
the illuminations of the salamander.

Now that my father's been given a second chance,
I'll stop arsing about with proper science
and make a science of impropriety:
stop worrying about what my ancestors
would think about the product of their germ cells;
let other sons do the double-blind studies;
drop the slide rule, pick up the bells and sceptre,
and, doing what I can do, do it well.

7

But I can't use his methodologies:
as much as I feel desperate to be
a cool logician or an abstract thinker,
a maker rather than a tinkerer,
those rules are murder to the pulse of verse
(as much as numbers rule its universe):
caution and pedantry are sensible
when handling a white-hot crucible –
but only literally. When I need
to hide my face from its own destiny
that's when I turn to him: I imitate
my father's faith that my balance is innate.
I imitate his fine brass weighing-scales,
fine enough to weigh him, and find him noble;
I weigh my father's wisdom in the balance
with the instability of my own sense,
trusting his bullion alloyed with my selves;
trusting that on his laboratory shelves
there's glassware, solvents, and procedures proven
to precipitate his good from my solution,
showing the half of him that's in my source code.
The rest's wormwood from his lab's nematodes,
wormwood, or cinnabar: pure mercury,
poison long peddled as a therapy
by the fast-fingered acolytes of Hermes
for love poorly expressed – for love's disease.

And this is why I fail: *he* is the balance,
not me. He has the unreactive valence,
while I'm the cation or anion,
compounding everything or everyone
I know, despite my own acidity.
I'm the hollow sword he filled with mercury;

I'm all in, past the tipping point, but trying
so hard to rein it in, to turn the stings
of my hard feelings into mellow songs
to hum as long as summer days are long,
or warm the wine set on a winter table.
I'm cursed with trying to seem capable.
I cannot be that voice. And if I try,
I may live longer but my heart will die;
there's no recollection in tranquillity
suited to codify this lust and fury –
that sounds ridiculous in measured verse
but not to try to say it would be worse.
Only the stent of form can hold the apse
of bloodlust up, can keep it from collapse.
I am my father's heart as it is now:
that rich red furrow cleared by a steel plough;
an echo of life's chaos, an unstable
turbulence of unreliable rhythms
beating to pace out the unpaceable,
beating to heal, to stitch over the schisms,
weak, strong, weak, strong, weak – and from now on, fated
to be artificially regulated.

I've become the dependent variable,
the unknown, possibly more noise than signal,
the plot against the research martinet's
meticulously plotted data-sets.
Father, that's all I am: a mind constrained
and self-created by its rhythm's feigned
orders, its pairs of matched neurotransmitter
transport mechanisms across a synapse
and their receptors – like a good rhyme's cantrips –
subjects for your pharmacology lectures
on beta-blockers and norepinephrine:
the chemical constraints on the machine,

measured words for the shocking things we feel,
words measured for, then sheathed in, a rhyme's steel
the way a nerve cell's sheathed in myelin
to keep the charge, to speed the name of action.
If neither of us were artificial men,
rhythmed by metal – metal-regulated –
I'm fairly certain that we'd both be dead.

8

All this love structures what must be returned,
all that he paid for that I never earned,
returned in reverence rhyming to excess –
of course excess, what grateful child does less? –
and rhythmed by such a heart. But I have done
less, and will do less than he did – succumbed
to the excesses that his measured pace
never permits: lust entering the race
for love and knowledge, so I'm now excessive
with both, not satisfied with what I have.

My gratitude for his ongoing 'I am',
his overtime, is a cardiogram
steadied by a lace of cobalt-chromium:
that bare, blood-surfing butterfly. The thrum
of pulse his heart sends through its flexing wings
harmonizes with this wild dithyramb:
rambling, drunk with relief. These words go whirling
at him, when their lines should lift his limbs
just as he lifted mine: with strength, but careful
not to exceed the reach of his control.
Instead they lie about what I perceive:
they're less than real, and less than I could heave
into my mouth if I could sugar-coat

the dose, or cloud the pane with anecdotes,
hiding my fear in his, or in the lie
that any of us are prepared to die.

But I'm willing to suspend my disbelief,
blend blood's suspension out of death and life;
I'll buy my own fictions, no harder than
buying that my father, blackout-born in Yatton,
born of the Filton works and the Anderson shelter,
when planes were made of wood, made by his father
(a carpenter – no, cabinet-maker, by trade)
this chemist's boy who grew into the wizard
chemist of epinephrine's shocking grasp,
this genial magus in his willow holdfast
is a space-age man. That steady in his chest
a printed-metal Psyche plays Antaeus,
Hal at the breach, Horatio at the bridge,
fence to the Fates, and to Death's door, a wedge:
a furling butterfly that spreads her wings
to press my father's arterial lining
and hold up all my hopes – the father figure
in me as it was formed, and will endure
as long as he's alive, and these illusions
can circulate between fathers and sons.
It's all that I can do; I've come to grips
with myself as a kind of psychic stent
keeping my father's, and my own, commandments,
keeping the heart's paths open, like an airstrip
for making aid drops till the crisis passes
(though we suspect the crisis may be endless),
till we both face the inescapable:
the folding of the wings, or the snipped soul
going where it can't know, and can't be known,
while all the cardiac muscle that we've grown
so slowly, almost imperceptibly,

twitches to its last electricity
as we perceive, too late, our mind's lost room:
the honey-dark of human death's cocoon
that breeds the maggot's beauty, that reverse
timelapse of Psyche's metamorphosis.

9

But all this talk's to talk away those odds:
this dream of death, this watchman's long aubade,
so long that it's become a serenade
or a nocturne, to a father out of bed.
It's the hard sell of cultists and their dupes,
General Patton cursing at his troops,
the chant of unrepentant monks and friars,
the boasts of narcissists and compulsive liars,
the mantras and the oversized pull-quotes
scattered by motivational speakers –
consolation that leaves the consoler weaker
when pitch and blurb can't keep their lives afloat.
It's the sales talk of wandering mendicants;
old fireside chat of pucks and fairy dances;
the quack's patter, the bromide-seller's charms;
my superstitions' firebreak against harm.
I see through all these, and my own cracked prism
thanks to my father's mild empiricism
that keeps me from believing what I write
even as I'm feeling it with all my might.

But here's how it hangs, gargoyle in marble hall,
the bare facts that console me best of all:
they stuck a stent into my father's arm,
swam it up over left or right atrium –
a cure I couldn't give him, so that I

am nothing more than his posterity,
dissolved, like plaque, into that stream of thought
that somehow carries on when we do not.
I'll help him live by living, by being alive,
and not by writing couplets that contrive
to explain things that didn't need explaining
or shrug them off with, *It never was a thing.*

I'm utterly content that he will last
longer, my love for him again surpassed
by his for me – adulthood's selfish stint,
the inner child still not taking the hint –
love leaving me with nothing more to wish for
but for the strength of a stent's mesh and wire,
and for the will to still be, when he isn't:
this space-age man, this alloyed harmony,
this cyborg grown out of a chemist's boy,
this symbiotic pulse of muscle and stent,
really the twin substance of any wish:
for Psyche's mettle married to the flesh.

He twists them out,
inverting each pale taper –
allows the prayer-drained flames

to gutter downwards
in brief obeisance
to some molten core,

then stubs each wick out
in the congealed lards
of the drip-tray –

he, the bored croupier
who shrugs, *'Les jeux sont faits...'*
and rakes the green felt sward.

NOTES & THANKS

ARES: According to a brief reference in the *Iliad* (5.385–91) the Aloadae (the giants Otus and Ephialtes) confined Ares inside a bronze *pithos,* or storage vessel, for a lunar year: 'Ares had to endure it when strong Ephialtes and Otos, / sons of Aloeus, chained him in bonds that were too strong for him, / and three months and ten he lay chained in the brazen cauldron...' (tr. Richard Lattimore, Chicago, 1951). He escaped with the help of Hermes and Artemis.

EMPUSA RED: Empusa: 'In classical mythology: a female demon or evil spirit associated with the goddess Hecate, supposed to eat humans and to be capable of appearing in different forms. ... "That same Empusa, of whom it is saide in Aristophanes ... she seemeth euery thing" [Miles Mosse, *The Arraignment and Conviction of Usurie* (London, 1595), iii. 60]' (*OED*).

DIORAMA: PRAIRIE SETTLERS IN A SOD HOUSE, 1900: The Red River cart was a large two-wheeled cart that exemplified simple, robust frontier technology; it was made entirely of wood and non-metallic materials. Like the York boats on Canadian waterways, the Red River carts proved indispensable to the fur trade in the early nineteenth century, hauling furs and other goods between St. Paul, Minnesota and Winnipeg, Manitoba. See Gilman, Gilman, and Stultz, *The Red River Trails: Ox-cart Routes between St. Paul and the Selkirk Settlement* 1820–1870 (Minnesota Historical Society, 1979).

A DOZEN ON THE HALF-SHELL: 7.ii: Yomi: the Japanese underworld. Susa-no-O: the Shinto god of the sea and storms, brother to the sun-goddess Amaterasu. 9: 'The boatmen and clam-diggers arose early and stopt for me, / I tuck'd my trowser-ends in my boots and went and had a good time; / You should have been with us that day round the chowder-kettle.' Walt Whitman, *Leaves of Grass* iii. 10.8–10.

THE SYCORAX QUIZ: The *Maschinenmensch* (lit. 'machine-person') was one of the first humanoid robots depicted on film, played by Brigitte Helm in Fritz Lang's *Metropolis* (1927). The film's female android was brought to life in an early special effects sequence in which horizontal rings of light surrounded her body. Some debate persists as to how exactly this effect was created.

NOJIRI HOPPER: The Nojiri hopper is the local name for the Emma field cricket, a brown cricket (エンマコオロギ) with long antennae, often seen around Lake Nojiri, Nagano Prefecture. Since the Meiji period, foreign missionaries have sought refuge from the summer heat at Karuizawa and Lake Nojiri. The *kokusaimura* (international village) at Nojiri still exists today.

LELANTOS THE HUNTER: The tales of Llyr were created by Leo Critchley.

YŌKAI: AKANAME ('FILTH LICKER'): *Yōkai* (妖怪) is the collective name for traditional Japanese monsters, ghosts, demons, and other supernatural phenomena. The *akaname* (垢嘗) was first illustrated by Toriyama Sekien in the *Gazu Hyakki Yagyō* (1776). *O-furo* (お風): a traditional Japanese-style bath tub. *Watabokori* (綿ぼこり): dustballs, fluff. *Sentō* (銭湯) a traditional public bath. *Onsen* (温泉): Japanese hotspring baths and resorts.

THE STENT: 1 'like "arrow" in the *kanji* for physician'. The first *kanji* in 'physician', *isha* (医者), shows the radical for dart or arrow inside a box, which might metaphorically represent a surgical tool or device inside a body with a wound or surgical opening. 3 *Shigane* and *hagane*: Japanese swords such as *katana* are made from *tamahagane*, steel produced through traditional smelting techniques. Swordmakers forge different blades depending on their individual folding and welding styles. *Hagane* is the hardest kind of sword-steel, and always forms the blade's cutting edge. *Shigane* is the softest sword-steel, sometimes used in the sides and spine of the blade, or in some blades not at all. *Kusanagi-no-Tsurugi* (草薙剣): the 'Grass-cutting Sword', a legendary two-edged sword taken by the god Susa-no-O from the body of the eight-headed serpent Yamata-no-Orochi (*Kojiki* i.18). *Ken* (剣): the general Japanese word for sword (and in particular, a *tsurugi* or double-edged sword, as opposed to a single-edged blade like the *katana*, which developed later). 8 'born of the Filton works and the Anderson shelter'. Filton was the home of the Bristol Aerospace Company, a major target for the Luftwaffe in 1940. A raid on the morning of 25 September 1940 killed 91 employees and delayed the development of the Bristol Beaufighter. (James Simons, one of the building crew for the first Beaufighter, survived the raid.) Anderson Shelters were prefabricated, above-ground air-raid shelters, named after the Home Secretary Sir John Anderson.

THANKS

I would like to thank Paul Rossiter for his meticulous reading and re-reading of these poems, which improved them immeasurably. Leo Critchley and William Demiri-Watson provided inspiration for, and criticism of, many of the book's ideas. The book would not have come into existence at all without Evelyn Rose Burrett, whose labour and love made available the hours and days during which these poems could be written and revised. Finally, the influence on these poems of Tina Burrett's wit, inspiration, and close reading and listening cannot be overstated. The passion and gratitude I feel for our life together cannot be expressed in prose, and demand better verse than any in these pages:

> *From Tina's eyes this doctrine I derive:*
> *They sparkle still the right Promethean fire;*
> *They are the books, the arts, the academes,*
> *That show, contain and nourish all the world:*
> *Else none at all in ought proves excellent.*